I0004630

Open Source

By Solis Tech

Understanding Open Source From the Beginning!

2nd Edition

Open Source (2nd Edition): Understanding Open Source from the Beginning!

Table Of Contents

Introduction

I want to thank you and congratulate you for downloading the book, *"Open Source: Understanding Open Source From the Beginning!"*

This book contains the basics in understanding the open source concept. What is it all about? Where did it come from? Who creates the open source content? How can software be considered as an 'open source'? What makes it different from the other software that we already have?

These questions are answered in this book. Also included in this book are information relevant to open source, such as examples of licensing, the Four Freedoms of free software use, and ideas about software piracy. This information will help to further understand what it means to have somesoftware that is open sourced.

Real life comparisons are also made in this book in case you become confused or lost in understanding the open source concept. The idea of open source seems very simple, but in reality, it is very complex, with definitions coinciding with the definitions of other concepts such as free software (which will further be discussed in Chapter Two). Listed down in the book are the advantages and disadvantages of open source software, and the reasons why more and more people are becoming enticed with the idea of converting to open source.

If the present generation already dictates the movement of open source software, what will become of it in the future? This question is also answered in the last chapter of this book. Due to the fast-paced advancement of technology, open source will adapt to this advancement with the help of both developers and users.

Thanks again for downloading this book, I hope you enjoy it!

Chapter 1: The Basics of Open Source

Have you ever wondered how an application you're using works? Every time you use an application and it freezes, do you think about what could have gone wrong? Do you ever think of why applications are constantly updating? These are questions that you would not be asked often. But these questions are very important to you, as a user of the Internet age.

Application programs are comprised of source codes, and these source codes are made by programmers. These codes are what allow you to type words into a word processing document, or to click on that video of cats meowing simultaneously. What you see onscreen are only visual representations of the codes of the program. Your application programs maybe paid, or pre-installed in your devices, so you don't have permission to view these codes. Rather, you get the pre-made product, and you as a consumer have no power over it except to use it as instructed.

When you purchase or download an application and place it in your device, it installs a lot of files, but none of these files contain the source code. A software manager is included in your installed files to monitor the application as you use it. Whenever your application gets bugged or freezes, this software manager runs, and it prompts you to file a report to the software's developers to tell them exactly what happened. Once the report is filed, the developers study the bug, fix it, and release an update a few days or weeks later.

But what if you could see these codes for yourself? What if, whenever something goes wrong with the application, you could easily contact the developers or ask for help from other programmers easily? These questions are the foundations of open source, and you are about to learn more about it in the following chapters.

What is Open Source?

Open source is a computer program that has its source code visible to the public. The public – which we can refer to as the users – have the power to view, copy, and modify the source codes to their liking. The source code and the compiled version of the code are distributed freely to the users without fixed fees. Users of open source can pretty much do anything they like with the open source programs that they downloaded, since there are practically no restrictions.

To better understand the concept of open source software, let us use an example of recipes for comparison.

Recipes start off with someone writing them down on a piece of paper. A grandma, perhaps, has a recipe for a cake, which she writes in her recipe book. She passes on this recipe to her children, and tells them that they can use the recipe whenever they like. But, they must make sure to credit her as the original creator of the recipe.

The children recreate the recipe and whenever they are asked where the recipe is from, they would always tell that it's from grandma. One of grandma's children alters the cake recipe by adding strawberries as an extra ingredient. The grandma allows this, given that she is also permitted to use the altered recipe.

This example has the same concept with open source software.

When a programmer writes a code, compiles it into a program, and distributes both the source code and the compiled program to the users, he is giving everyone permission to access everything about the program. Users can run the program, view the code, modify if needed, compile, and redistribute the modified version of the program.

The original programmer, however, would require the users to let him use the modified versions of his program, since it is his to begin with. Aside from this certain restriction, the users of the program have the freedom to do whatever they like to do with it.

Let's go back to the example of the cake recipe. One of grandma's children, the one who added the strawberries, suggests to grandma to add the strawberries to the original recipe. The grandma thinks that this is a good idea therefore she complies and replaces her old recipe with the altered cake recipe.

In open source software, if the programmer is notified of a certain modification of a user, and it is deemed to be a modification that the software needs, then the programmer will revise his program based on that certain modification. This modification is called a patch. The user who has suggested of the modification is now coined as a contributor. This process of adapting user modification to an open source software is called upstreaming, because the modification goes back to the original code.

The concept of open source depends on the communication and collaboration between the software's developers and its users. Bug detection and fixing of open source is made easier because numerous users are working simultaneously to study the source code and to compile a modified, fixed version of the code.

With open source, it is not only the developers who are finding new ways on how the software can be improved and upgraded. The users can also contribute their ideas and knowledge in the upgrading of the software. The original developer or programmer can be called the maintainer who monitors the changes in his or her original software.

Let us then go back to the cake recipe. What if another child of grandma decides to do his own version of the cake recipe? He adds raisins to the cake recipe, and asks grandma if the raisins can be added with the strawberries in the original recipe. Grandma refuses, because she dislikes raisins. Instead of being disheartened, this child decides that he would create his own version of the recipe and share it with the people he knows.

If a certain modification makes no appeal to the developer, the one who suggested the modification may opt to make his own version of the program. This act of not patching a modification from the original program is called forking. A forked program is a certain program that alters the original program in such a way that it becomes its own program.

A forked program can be described as a chip off an old block, since it doesn't necessarily separate itself from the license of the program it originated from, although it may seem like it due to the avoidance of patching. Programmers that collaborate with open source result to forking if their modified versions of the original program are deemed unfit by the program's developer.

Nonprofit organizations are the prime developers of open source software. However, due to the freedom of customization that open source has given both users and developers, even large companies are adhering to the open source culture.

How did Open Source become popular?

During the early times of computing, software followed a protocol and design with everyone conforming to a certain cookie-cutter ideal. Software was yet to be imagined as cost-free, and the developers kept their codes to themselves. But then, during the early 90's, the idea of sharing one's code to the public became an accepted idea to most users. The concept of software being free and open sourced became a reality when, after decades, the likes of Mozilla Firefox and OpenOffice were created.

Open source rose in its ranks when developers started making open source alternatives of commercial software. These alternatives are free and can easily be downloaded from the internet, enticing most users to convert to open source. What made open source rise, however, was the idea of community. Fellow programmers could interact and communicate with each other, and even with the developers, which was unheard of during the early times of computing. People could collaborate with the developers of the software and share their insights.

Open source has also given its users the freedom to fully inspect software before they use it – an action that was impossible to do with closed source software. Users who are into coding try open source and study the code line by line.

The popularity of open source software has been anticipated due to the fact that a lot of people supported the cause. Programmers started creating open source projects to contribute to the cause, and users started to get accustomed to obtaining and downloading open source software. With volunteers signing up left and right, and organizations creating their own programs, the growth and expansion of open source software cannot be stopped anymore.

Chapter 2: History, Comparisons, and Relevance

Open source was not immediately implemented until the early 90's, where more and more people began to realize the importance of being able to share the source code of software without fees and royalties. Like any other idea, open source started out as a small thought of making software free for the public, and grew into the culture that it is today.

The History of Open Source: The Open Source Initiative

Eric Raymond, an American software developer, published an essay (turned book) entitled The Cathedral and the Bazaar in 1997. The essay speaks about two different types of software, which he labels the Cathedral and the Bazaar.

In the essay, Raymond describes the Cathedral to be the type of software in which with each release of software, the source code of the software will be available. However, with each build of the software, the certain code block that has been modified is restricted to only the developers of the software. The examples presented under the Cathedral type of software were GNU Emacs (a type of text editor) and the GNU Compiler Collection (a compiler that caters to different programming languages).

In contrast, the Bazaar is the type of software that has the Internet as the venue for their development, making the code visible to the public. The example presented under the Bazaar type of software was Linux (now a widely known computer operating system), in which Raymond coined the developer Linus Torvalds to be the creator of the Bazaar type of software.

Raymond's article became popular in 1998, getting the attention of major companies and fellow programmers. Netscape was influenced by this article, leading them to release the source codes of their internet suite called Netscape Communicator. The source code of the said internet suit was what gave birth to internet browsers such as Thunderbird and SeaMonkey. Mozilla Firefox, a popular web browser today, was also based from the source codes of Netscape Communicator.

The idea of source codes being free became widespread when Linux was developed, urging people to contribute to the open source cause. Because of the increasing popularity of Linux and similar projects, people who became interested in the cause formed the Open Source Initiative, a group whose advocacy is to tell people about the benefits of open sourcing and why it is needed in the computing world.

Open Source vs. Free Software

Most people confused open source software with free software, as the two terms share somewhat the same advocacy. With understanding, it is not that difficult to tell these two terms apart.

The difference between free software and open source software can be listed down into different points. Although they have their differences, both free software and open source software have a singular goal – to publicize source codes for the users to see.

Free software focuses mainly on the ethical aspect of the advocacy. There are certain freedoms that free software are fighting for when it comes to the use of software, which cannot be given to the users by commercial software. These are the Four Freedoms of software use according to advocates of free software:

• The freedom to use the software. This means that the user is free to use the software to his or her needs, or as instructed.

• The freedom to study the source codes of the software. Since the codes are readily available for public viewing, the user has the freedom to view and study the said codes. After he or she reviews the codes, he or she then has the freedom to do the next step.

• The freedom to modify the source codes of the software to the user's liking. If necessary, the user has the freedom to customize the source code and to create a version of the program fit for the user's specific needs.

• The freedom to share the modified, compiled source codes to the public. If the program has been modified, the user has the freedom to compile and publish the modified program for the benefit of the other users who may also have the need of the program's modification. The developer of the original program should also be given the freedom and right to use the modified version of the program.

Free software allows its users to do whatever they want with a program. If they want to modify the source code and redistribute the modified code as their own, without the consent of the original developers, then they are free to do so. If the user wishes to use the source code as the base code of a new project that they are working on, then they will not be sued. The ethical reasoning of free software simply states that there are no grave restrictions when it comes to copying, revising, and republishing the already existing software.

Open source, on the other hand, creates programs with the Four Freedoms in mind. The programs which are considered open source are made for the user's convenience and benefit. The common idea of open source is a group of people working on a single open source project, attempting to create a program that will be beneficial to them, as well as the users.

Open Source and Paid Software

Open source software did indeed come from paid software. There are countless of open source alternatives for common, commercially-sold software readily available on the internet. Some examples of this are office suites like LibreOffice and OpenOffice, which are open source alternatives for the much more popular Microsoft Office.

The reason why open source alternatives of paid software exist is mainly the cost. Users would opt to pay less, or none at all, for certain software. Why pay for software when there are free alternatives that can be downloaded from the internet easily? Open source makes it possible for users who cannot afford paid software to experience the basic and intermediate features of the software, without sacrificing the quality of the end product.

Although open source may be the overall solution for users to get a feel of certain software, there are still others who would want to obtain paid software but through illegal means. This is called software piracy, an action that is still evident despite it being illegal in most countries.

Software piracy is the act of downloading or installing a paid software illegally, either through software cracks or illegally burned CDs. The most popular way to obtain pirated software is through downloading Torrent-based software crack, in which the user can get the files through different computers almost discreetly. Since these software are pirated, installing these software requires the user to turn off his or her Internet connection before installing, to avoid being tracked.

Some paid software can be bought once, and shared with different computers or devices. All of the information regarding the sharing of paid software can be found on the software's End User License Agreement or EULA. The EULA is a splash screen shown at the start of the software's installation which contains the contract between the software's developers and the user.

The EULA may allow the user to share one copy of the software to different devices, or it may restrict the user from doing so. Once the user has violated this part of the EULA, it can then be considered as software piracy.

Something that a user should be aware of is a certain license called the GNU General Public License, the license that most open source software adhere to. The license permits the user to copy, modify, and redistribute the modified code, just as long as the source files and the original codes are still documented. This is important in understanding how and why open source software is allowed to move freely across the internet without being coined as software piracy, as compared to paid, propriety software.

With propriety or paid software, the user is buying only the license. He is not allowed to revise the code, to reverse-engineer the code, and to view the code by all means. The only thing that the user is allowed to do when he purchases propriety software is to use a copy of the software that the developer has provided. It may seem like an unfair deal to some people, because a user should be able to own something that he has paid for.

Open source software changes that idea. It gives the user the freedom to see the program's source code, letting the user know the program's 'skeletal system'. Even without paying for the software, the user gets the full potential functions of the software and not just an executable copy of it.

Importance of Open Source

Technology is rapidly changing. Experts are coming up with more ways to improve the lives of other people. It is the same with those who contribute to open source projects. Their advocacy is to create free programs that will benefit the users.

Open source is important in the evolution of quality software. With a lot of people contributing to one singular project, the software that is produced will be the best of its kind as it has been meticulously observed and reviewed by the contributors. Open source gives way for the collaborative effort of different programmers and users, with the users being secondary developers of a certain program. It is an interactive effort, with the users being able to update the program alongside the developers themselves.

The fast paced advancement of technology would often overwhelm content creators to the point that they would stop creating content altogether. Content creators who are left behind by technology's advancement are often working in small groups or on their own, and have no means of help from fellow creators of their kind.

With Open source, this is never the case. Each open source software has its own community to back a fellow programmer up during each build, ready to help out other programmers and users when needed. The open source community's bond with each other is what makes open source catch up with the fast advancement of technology.

Chapter 3: The Benefits and the Downsides of Open Source

The Benefits of Open Source

The most obvious perk of having open source software is the availability of the source code. With the source code available to the general public, people are able to study the code line by line. Students of programming can study the source code and implement some blocks of it into their own projects, honing their skills and improving their code. Users who are meticulous with their software can view the codes and customize the said codes to their liking.

Aside from the source codes being publicized, another perk of having open source software is that it is mostly free, depending on the software's license. Users of open source software do not have to pay a large sum of money to be able to enjoy the full functions of the software. If the license requires the user to pay, the user may still try out the software's full functions before purchasing.

Open source promotes community. If a user encounters a problem with the downloaded software, he or she can seek help from fellow programmers or the developers themselves through a forum. Users and programmers alike can communicate and share their experiences with using the software, helping other users to get used to the software. With other programmers keen on editing and revising the source code, updated and better versions of the software can easily be uploaded and shared within the community for the benefit of the other users.

Also, when something goes wrong with the open source software, the user has the option to fix the problem himself should seeking help be an option that is not convenient for him. In propriety software, this cannot be possible as the license and copyright prohibits its users from ever touching the program's source code.

If the user of propriety software does as much as reverse-engineer the product, then they could be violating the program's copyright and therefore, be taken to jail. Open source software removes this restriction from the users, giving them permission to fix solvable program problems on their own.

The benefits of open source software are not limited to personal use. Companies and businesses are adhering to the open source paradigm due to the endless possibilities at half the price or lesser.

More and more businesses are converting to open source mainly because it is more cost-efficient than purchasing commercial software. Companies also have more freedom with open source software in terms of customization, since they have the power to mold the software to fit their company's needs. These factors are beneficial in the growth and development of businesses in such a way that the businesses need not to put out a large sum of money just to be able to acquire a software that will be utilized in their business.

Open sourcing has become a way for people to have access to the things that they initially did not have access to. Users of software now have the ability to study the source code of the program they are using, and to know how exactly a certain function of the program runs by looking at its specific line of code.

A sense of community is also created between the software's developers and programmers from outside of their firms. Through open sourcing, the developers are able to communicate with other programmers with regards to how the software can be enhanced further.

Some users would say that using open source operating systems grants more security as compared to paid operating systems. For example, if a user installs the Linux operating system, he or she does not need an antivirus or a virus detection software to keep his or her files intact. The operating system itself has security measures for the user. This becomes a benefit for both professional and nonprofessional users because they have more room for important files rather than installing different kinds of applications for protection.

Open source software is made for the people, by the people. It hones itself to the needs and wants of each user. Because of this, there is no need for the user to upgrade his or her hardware every time the software upgrades.

Take Apple's OSX (operating system) for example. Certain updates of the operating system are available to download, with better features than the previous build. However, older versions of the Macbook and the iMac cannot avail of the recent builds as their hardware are not fit enough to accommodate either the size of the downloaded file or the features itself.

With open source software, the upgrades can be coded to fit each user's needs, depending on the user's hardware. If a certain upstreamed version of the open source software is available to download, different downloaders are made available by the developer with the specifications listed beside each downloader, catering to the different specifications of the user. The user himself can opt to customize the code of the program to be compatible with his device.

Having the right to use the Open Source software in any way they want has also enticed users to use it more regularly. Likewise, such right has attracted the attention of people, especially those who are quite skeptic to try it. After all, people are more inclined to use something when they are given rights of use as well as redistribution rights. Aside from users, more developers have also been encouraged to use, modify, and develop it. Because of this, the Open Source software gets the opportunity to improve in functionality and quality.

Allowing the user these freedoms over the software has given open source software a bit of a leverage over paid, propriety software. But then again, there will be nay-sayers who think that open source software isn't the way to go.

The Downsides and Disadvantages of Open Source

Open sourcing has given users lots of benefits, but it is not perfect. Some would still prefer paid software over any open sourced software. Here are some of the reasons why some users do not approve of open source.

If a user is not in any way a technology expert, he or she would want software that is easy to use. Open source software is known to be more technical compared to their paid counterparts. Paid software focuses on its user interface, making the application easy for the user to understand the system. Open source software usually start out with a not so attractive user interface, but with the basic functions of the program intact. As the program gets updated with each build, the user interface changes and adapts to the needs of its users.

Most critics would say that paid or propriety software is still better in a number of factors as compared to open source software. Because more people are accustomed to using paid or propriety software, the idea that there are other types of software available is intimidating to them. People think that open source software is made only for the technology savvy users, with the interface hard for them to manipulate. Why download a complicated software when they can buy a simple, pre-made software that they are already familiar with?

Paid software has become a norm in the everyday lives of users. Large companies such as Microsoft and Apple have made their name known all throughout the world, creating technologies that users and consumers have grown to love. Because of their undying popularity, the rise of open source software is unknown to the general public. And even if they are known, those who are used to seeing the big names are hesitant to try out what open source might be.

Seeking technical help might seem simple with the numerous open source communities readily available, but it may sometimes be inconvenient to the user. Paid software offer professional tech support straight from the manufacturers.

Moreover, Open Source is vulnerable to malicious users. Since it is accessible by anyone, it may fall into the hands of people with bad intentions. These people may use the software to exploit its vulnerabilities and develop bugs that corrupt hardware or steal vital information. Such drawbacks do not often occur with commercially produced software because they undergo stringent quality control processes to ensure that they are just about perfect before they are released to the public.

With this being said, Open Source solutions may not be as reliable as their commercially-produced counterparts. While it is true that huge multinational companies such as Sun Microsystems and IBM currently support the Open Source software movement, it still cannot be denied that there are plenty of risks involved with regard to its reliability. There is really no huge financial stake and their motivation mainly comes from being "anti-Microsoft."

There isn't a clear cut discipline in the industry. Everything is driven by emotions. The promoters and developers of free source software still believe in the idealistic and obscure world in which there are no intellectual property rights and that software companies do not produce commercial software. This is why it is not possible to run any major business operations on these products.

Aside from not being as user friendly as its commercially available counterparts, Open Source software also does not come with an extensive customer support. The moment you decide to go for Open Source, you are practically on your own. While you can always turn to the Internet for help and guidance, it is still not the same with commercial software wherein you can call a hotline and receive personalized support.

The self-motivated forums and tutorials available online are still no match for actual customer support. When you use Open Source, you need to find out by yourself how to use and install applications without damaging your hardware and losing vital data. You cannot find any manuals or documents for the software since it is frequently modified. In case your hardware is damaged or your program does not function properly, there is no one you can hold liable.

With commercially available software, you know exactly who the developer and manufacturer are. You know exactly who to contact or even sue in case things go downhill. With Open Source, however, the software is modified by numerous individuals. So as a user, you cannot exactly pinpoint to a specific person or entity in case something goes wrong.

Furthermore, you may be discouraged from using Open Source due to its high costs of installation. A lot of people have this misconception that they can save more money if they use Open Source solutions. In fact, about 99% of laptop and desktop computers have a pre-installed Windows OS. Unfortunately, only a handful of Open Source applications are compatible with this operating system. Likewise, most of these applications are not compatible with high-tech electronic devices.

With regard to updates, Open Source does not provide any guarantee. After all, nobody is legally bound to provide you with updates on a regular basis. You can actually be stuck with your old version without getting a new one ever. Then again, this may not be such a huge drawback anyway.

Chapter 4: The Open Source Culture

Open source gives the user freedom to do whatever he or she wants in a software. Who wouldn't want the freedom to edit source codes to their own liking? With open source, this opportunity of customization is available at hand.

Why are more people converting to open source?

With the source code open for public scrutiny, looking for errors will be easier. Other software companies that do not have their source code publicized have their own set of programmers and developers figuring out the bugs in the software. This is an advantage for companies who always require their software to be updated regularly to keep up with the business.

Students who cannot afford the luxury of paid software turn to their open source counterparts to be able to utilize their functions without having to pay a large amount of money. Open source alternatives of Microsoft Office are available for the students to download should they need to use an office suite for their projects.

Some open source versions of paid software are actually better. Paid media players can play certain file types and extensions, but crash once the file extension is unrecognizable. Open source software developers take note of these bugs and create a media player that can play almost all media file types and extensions in high definition. Because of this, even users who are not actually technology savvy would convert to the open source alternatives of paid software just because they've heard and they know that they can get more out of the open source counterpart.

Programmers who want to practice their coding also rely on readily available open source software in their study. Because the codes of open source can easily be viewed and modified, programmers can base their project on open source software and publish it as their own, creating a program fork.

Businesses, on the other hand, turn to open source software for two main factors: cost efficiency and the power of customization. As mentioned in a previous chapter, with open source software readily available to download on the internet, the businesses do not need to spend a lot of money for a software that they cannot customize as their own. Open source gives them the opportunity to keep on upgrading their system as needed, therefore improving the quality of their software with each build.

The flexibility of open source software has enticed businesses to change to open source from propriety software. Businesses would often buy already existing software and attempt to use them as instructed by the developers. Open source software has its own rules and regulations, but if businesses want their software to be something specific, then the developers of open source software will deliver. With propriety software, the business is the one to adjust to the software that they have purchased, an action that is removed once businesses convert to open source.

Examples of Open Source Software

A wide variety of open source software are available for download. These software may be used for utility purposes, for multimedia purposes – anything that the user desires and requires. Here are a few examples of open source software that you as a user have probably heard of.

The prime example of open source software is an operating system called Linux. It is an operating system based off of UNIX that is available to different computer platforms and hardware.

Another example of open source software is the media player called VLC Media Player developed by the VideoLAN Organization. This media player can run a variety of multimedia files at high definition. Its paid counterpart is Microsoft's own Windows Media Player, which before its most recent build can only play a handful of file extensions.

When it comes to operating systems, Android is another popular example of open source software. A company called Android, Inc. (later bought by Google) has developed this mobile operating system using another open source kernel, Linux. It caters mostly to devices which have touchscreen on them, such as touchscreen desktop monitors, tablets, and smartphones, much like its counterpart from Apple called iOS. Android has its own application store called Google Play, where the users can install applications onto their phones mostly for free.

Netbeans, a well-known software developing application, is also an example of an open source software. It is a Java-created application that caters to different programming languages, and can be run on multiple operating systems. Programmers use Netbeans to create object oriented applications using the 24 programming languages that it caters to.

GIMP, or GNU Image Manipulation Program, is an Adobe Photoshop-like application that edits photos and creates graphic images. It has basic photo editing features such as cropping, grayscaling, and resizing, making it a simpler alternative to Photoshop. Like its paid counterpart, users of GIMP can also create animated GIF images, a feature that most multimedia artists are very fond of using.

Video and computer games can also be open sourced. Some open source games such as Tux Racer are available in the Linux package when downloaded. The principle of open source games is the same as any other open source software – the developers merging and collaborating with the users to create quality content to be distributed to the general public. However, the visual quality and elements of open source games are yet to be improved.

Other examples include PHP (a web development language), MySQL (used in databases alongside applications such as Microsoft Access and Microsoft Visual Basic), Python (programming language), Blender (an Autocad Maya-esque application that caters to 3D rendering), and many more.

Chapter 5: The Future of Open Source

What will happen in the future?

The future of open sourcing seems bright. With most businesses converting to open source software and most developers contributing to open source projects, the growth and expansion of open sourcing will continue. Open sourcing gives way for the innovation of modern software technology – with a lot of people working on one simple open source project, there is no doubt that the project will continue to be updated and improved.

Software will only continue to improve as time passes by. Open source software has made it easier for software to improve and upgrade itself due to countless of volunteers who are up to the challenge. While propriety software claim to start software trends, open source software advocates the upgrades of software that will be favorable to the needs of the users rather than to the bank accounts of the developers.

Open source software does not wish to waste the time and money of the user; rather, it aims to maximize both time and money, with the inclusion of effort, of the user when utilizing the software.

Presently, paid software are still dominant over open source software. Paid software have more leverage compared to open source software when it comes to reliability and familiarity, since they have been used by programmers and users alike for decades. There is still a certain percentage of users who are not aware that there are open source versions of their paid software, which they can help improve and customize to their own needs and liking.

More people will be aware of the benefits of open source software in the future. With propriety software releasing more licenses that restrict its users from certain software freedom, the existence of open source will lead to the users converting from propriety software due to the lack of free will.

In the future, there is a possibility that open source will be available not just for software, but also for other forms of content that have sources.

The future of open source as an idea or a paradigm will not be restricted to software alone. With the further advancement of technology, more and more gadgets will be locked down by licenses and warranties which restrict its users from fixing even simple problems that the product may have.

Gadgets are becoming more and more digitized, and copyright restricts people from ever touching or attempting to change the software. Because of this, some people are beginning to open up to the idea of open source not just for software, but also for hardware and gadgets that are used every day.

Let us take tractors for example. Tractors are machines that are essential in farming. If a tractor breaks down, the farmer himself can fix the broken tractor and keep it running again without having to buy a new one. But the modernization of technology leads the manufacturers of tractors to add digital aspects into their products: tractors now have microchips and are operated via computers, therefore are now protected by copyright.

Now, if the new tractor breaks down, the farmer has no permission to fix the tractor himself. He must hire a specialist to fix the problem, or else he goes to jail.

Open source hardware has already started to rise in its ranks alongside open source software. It basically means that users are free to create their gadgets from scratch, using open source hardware. Although the idea seems taboo at present, the fact that gadgets are also being restricted from the users will give way for both open source hardware and software to rise even further, giving users complete freedom over the creation and implementation of the technology that they need.

Content creators are restricted from creating certain things just because of copyright laws. Even artists, who upload videos on websites like YouTube and Vimeo, get flagged just because of a certain song or a certain speech that had some sort of copyright over it. This restricts creative freedom.It also restricts the content creators from creating what they know and love, and sharing it with their viewers.

Will open sourcing become a culture in the future? Surely, with the massive amounts of information available for the users to share freely amongst themselves. Open source software has given way for an idea that will change the world of computing for everyone, and allows everyone to have access to the large chunk of information that was previously not available to them. Transparency when it comes to creating code and building machines will become a fad in the future, as more and more people are willing and able to create content and share it with other users.

Open Source, Then and Now

In 2014, it was reported that 56% of companies and businesses expect to back up more open source projects. As of May 2015, it was reported that 78% of these companies and businesses claim that they run operations using Open Source solutions. Every year, interesting developments with regard to the perception and adoption of Open Source are revealed.

According to the Future of Open Source Survey, Open Source has attained unprecedented pervasiveness levels in 2015. This survey has analyzed the input and feedback of professionals in the information technology industry. Open Source, which was once considered as a novelty, has now gained more respect from businesses. In fact, only 3% of companies admitted that they do not use Open Source in running their business.

This is indeed a significant increase in its usage and popularity. All of this has happened in such a short span of time. Within the last five years, this statistics has actually doubled. Companies, whether small or big, are starting to grasp the advantages that Open Source software solutions have to offer. They are starting to appreciate and use it for their business. This is a far cry from what survey reports revealed in 2007, when a majority of the companies thought of Open Source as merely a gimmick.

Open Source has come a long way. Today, it has proven that startup software vendors do not have to produce closed source products and services alone in order to be successful. It is clear and obvious that Open Source is a default base when it comes to software development for it has infiltrated a large facet of modern enterprises. It has even outperformed proprietary software on security, cost, quality, and customization.

Furthermore, it has been found that successful businesses are those that make use of Open Source solutions. A lot of traditional leaders in information technology have also realized the benefits that open source offers and the drawbacks that proprietary software has.

Sample Findings According to the Survey

- According to survey reports, 78% of the respondents stated that their businesses run a portion or all of their operation on Open Source software. Such finding has actually doubled within five years. In 2010, only 42% of these companies said that they would use Open Source in running their businesses or any other information technology environment.
- 93% of the respondents also stated that their organizations make use of Open Source and that they have either increased or maintained the same level of usage within the past year.
- At present, 64% of companies are actively participating in projects related to Open Source. This number has actually increased from just 50% in 2014.
- For the next two to three years, it is expected that 88% of companies would increase their contribution and participation to projects run on Open Source software.
- More than 66% of the companies that responded to the survey stated that they consider Open Source as a better option than others when it comes to selecting a default approach on software.
- 58% of companies believe that Open Source is more affordable than any other software solution. In fact, they believe that it actually affords the best ability to scale.

- 43% of companies stated that Open Source software offers better ease of deployment than proprietary software solutions.
- 55% of companies believe that Open Source gives a better security than proprietary software solutions. It is even expected for Open Source security to increase to 61% within two to three years.
- 45% of the respondents stated that Open Source solutions are considered to be a better option when it comes to choosing a solution for evaluating security technology for internal use.
- Indeed, Open Source participation has given a competitive advantage to enterprises. 65% even stated that it enables enterprises to compete against one another and win. This percentage has increased from only 45% back in 2014.
- 39% of cloud computing, 35% of big data, 33% of operating systems, and 31% of the Internet of Things are said to be highly affected by Open Source and such numbers are expected to grow within the next two to three years.
- Half or 50% of the respondents stated that Open Source software has helped them find and acquire the best talents. It is a known fact that the competition for talent in the information technology industry has grown for all companies of different sizes. With this being said, Open Source solutions should not be disregarded or overlooked.

Perhaps the best part of the survey reports is the future forecasts. Open Source is still in the initial stages and has the ability to influence industries and change the way they work. With it being able to reach new levels of ubiquity and pervasiveness, its potential increases. It can actually result in billions of dollars being generated in the years to come.

Chapter 6: Open Source Policy

The Open Source policy currently has a version that was published in 2004 and restated in 2009. This restated policy aims to make sure that taxpayers get the most of their money.

It reflects changes in the approach of the government towards information technology and the Open Source market. It requires that there be a level playing field for Open Source software. In addition, it encourages the usage of open standards as well as the re-use of purchased software solutions.

This current Action Plan of the government lays out the steps necessary for it to be accomplished. Moreover, it gives instructions to the suppliers of information technology to make the most of Open Source.

So what are the main points of this policy?

- The government fairly and actively considers Open Source solutions along with other proprietary software products when it comes to making decisions of procurement.
- These procurement decisions are based on money value. Whatever gives businesses the best value for their money is chosen. Also, the total cost of solution ownership, including transition and exit costs, are taken into consideration. These factors are all evaluated after making sure that such solutions fulfill the essential and minimum capability, scalability, security, support, manageability, and transferability requirements.
- The government expects those who bring information technology solutions forward to develop a good mix of proprietary and open source products in order to make sure that the best overall solution is attained.
- Open Source is chosen based on added inherent flexibility where there's no significant cost different between non-open source and open source software solutions.

The government does not mandate the usage of open source software solutions for certain reasons. According to government representatives of the United Kingdom, procurement legislation deems open source mandating as an antitrust law breach. This is based on the interpretation that Open Source is either a feature or a product. Italy and other countries, for example, do not view Open Source as a product, but rather as a feature.

Because of this, Open Source preference has been a product's legal feature preference. There isn't any commercial vendor that has been disfavored or favored inappropriately. Mandating open source also precludes the option of commercially available software from procurement processes. It has not yet been proven categorically that open source actually offers better value for money with regard to the overall ownership cost.

Chapter 7: Myths Surrounding Open Source

Even though the current policy has been in existent since 2004, evidence shows that there is still very little open source software used by the government. In fact, there are a variety of myths that surround the software. Here are some of the most common myths about it:

- *Open Source is not very secure.*

  This is not true. One huge barrier to OSS consideration is the misapprehension that it inherently has a bigger risk compared to proprietary software. As you know, source code is readily available. This is why it is often viewed as a great risk in security. As a result, it has increased open source wariness in all the government departments.

  There are even people who fear that due to the availability of the source code to the public, the software is not very secure. They believe that it is much risker as compared to closed source solutions. Nevertheless, this is countered with the thousand eyes argument. According to this argument, the code accessibility promotes the early detection of vulnerabilities as well as encourages fixes that ultimately result in more secure products.

  Take note that there are numerous pros and cons for both the OSS and proprietary products. Both of them have certain vulnerabilities and may be prone to attacks. Just as with proprietary software, you can expect open source software to have both positive and negative examples.

  According to the current CESG Guidance, there is no particular kind of software that is inherently less or more secure than other types of software. Likewise, there is no particular kind of software that is more favorable than another. Every kind of software has to be approached differently, depending on their case. This means that a person cannot exclude open source solutions during evaluation just because they are perceived to be less secure.

Another common myth about open source is that departments should only use software products that are accredited. This is obviously a misunderstanding of the accreditation and security process. Keep in mind that whole solutions are accredited, not the products. These solutions consist of software products, information flows, configurations, users, mitigations against risks, and physical and other controls.

A set of limited functionality products is not assured by CESG. Also, these are security enforcing products, including cryptographic systems or firewalls. However, most of the software products that the government uses do not belong under this category. In addition, there is no reason why such assured products cannot be open source.

- *An open source solution cannot be acquired without any fee.*

This is also false because you can get open source software absolutely for free. Users can choose the most ideal level of services and support. You can find a market for paid-for services and support for common enterprise open source software. It is pretty common for system integrators to give their support to such providers.

Sometimes, it is even reasonable to make use of open source with no support at all. For instance, prototyping, pilots, and trials can make use of open source software with little to no support. This is one of the main advantages of this software solution.

Departments are required to take on a more sophisticated cost evaluation when it comes to the ownership of software products. A Total Cost of Ownership or TCO model takes several factors into consideration. This affects the total costs as well as the cost avoidance, which includes acquisition, integration, in-life changes, open standards and interoperability, technology lock-in dependency chains, exit costs, and multi-supplier market competition.

Remember that the practice of making unit price comparison does not take added sources of cost avoidance and cost into consideration. Business cases that involve TCO comparisons must also allocate weight for the alignment to policy and strategic aims.Say, for instance, when a solution option lowers the barriers to SME engagement, it has to be reflected in the option comparison, with the necessary weight.

- *Open Source is not licensed.*

Open Source is licensed. The software is actually defined by such license, but it is by terms of use. Unlike with proprietary software, the licenses are not by items bought. Proprietary software is protected by the laws on copyright. Open source is not exempted from this. Take note that there are certain obligations that come with using OSS. So before you download and use any source code or software application, see to it that you establish your license model for the software.

Keep in mind that there are various license models available for open source. Every one of these licenses has particular terms for the modification and use of code. Because of this, it is essential to take note of the open source license specifics as well as the way the department plants to redistribute and use any OSS modification.

The most common models include the following:

a. Apache License
b. Mozilla Public License (MPL)
c. BSD License
d. GNU Lesser General Public License (LGPL)
e. GPL versions 2 and 3

Legal and commercial professionals usually expect to see proprietary licenses that cover indemnity against any intellectual property infringement, limited liabilities, and performance warranties. The licenses for open source are not meant to cover such issues and are thereby addressed by support contracts or service contracts.

A lot of the licenses related to the Open Source software allow the modification of OSS for internal use. You can actually modify it even without distributing the source code and making it known to the public. Then again, if you decide to distribute your modified OSS in the market or outside of your organization, you have to remember that some licenses

27

require that the software recipient also becomes allowed to access the modified source code.

On the other hand, if you do not distribute the modified software outside of your organization, you will not be obliged to share such modified source code. This can give you better peace of mind with regard to security. Majority of the users of Open Source do not even modify the source code. They simply get the packaged components of the software from the suppliers that provide both services and support. Because of this, they experience issues with obligations as well as become responsible for managing any issues related to changes in the software.

- *Open Source is merely a fad.*

Open Source is not a fad. It is not even new. In fact, it has already been around and available for commercial purposes since the mid-1990s. At present, it is utilized by major organizations who run critical or large scale infrastructures. In addition, Open Source is used by organizations that prioritize security.

Take note that the term 'Open Source' was not used until 1998. However, some of its concepts have already been around since the 1980s. For instance, Copyleft, which is a concept developed by Richard Stallman, is used as an alternative to Copyright. It is meant to ensure that materials are allowed to be used, examined, copied, built upon, and adapted freely. The term was first used in 1985.

Then, in 1991, Linux Kernal was released by Linus Tovalds as a freely modifiable code. Within a couple of years, computers started to be sold with a pre-installed Linux operating system. Cabinet Office investigated Open Source for the first time in 2001 and 2002. During that time, it was deemed necessary to have a strict policy on OSS usage in the United Kingdom.

The policy's present version goes way back to 2004 and indicates how long the government has been trying to promote the use of Open Source solutions for cost effectiveness. This policy was stated again in 2009. It was actually restated in the Open Source, Open Standards and Re-Use: Government Action Plan because the implementation and engagement with OSS was not found to be as good as expected. Once again, the policy was refreshed in 2010.

Chapter 8: Frequently Asked Questions (FAQ)

There are a lot of questions related to the Open Source software. If you want to know more about this solution, the following questions and answers may be able to help you out:

What is going on with the Open Source software?

The government actually requires the active and fair consideration of open source solutions in businesses. They state that using such solutions offers the best value for your money. With this being said, the government hopes that using open source solutions would help result in a more competitive and fairer marketplace that has better direct opportunities for both small and medium-sized enterprises. The government commits to developing a level playing field for innovative ICT solutions, such as open source software. This is so supplier lock-in can be prevented and better value for money can be delivered.

What exactly is the Open Source software?

You have learned from the previous chapters what Open Source is and what it does. It is actually a software solution for which the source code rights as well as other available rights for copyright owners are readily accessed in the public domain, provided that they have a license. This license generally allows users to use, improve, or change the software if they want to offer it for redistribution. The Open Source software has a license that guarantees freedom to modify and access source codes; freedom to reuse and redistribute the software; freedom to use it in any way possible; and a responsibility to share any improvements built on other people's work.

Is being able to see and modify the source code crucial for a lot of people?

Yes, it is. While it is true that only a handful of people are in need of direct access to the source code, it is still essential that the business or customer is able to control the technology around which they build their business or company. Consider the proprietary software business. In this kind of business, customers do not have any control over it. The supplier is the one that has control over it. For instance, in the event that the supplier charges too much for the business, does not want to fix problems, or implements a certain change in which the business loses the option to deal with other suppliers, then it can be said that the supplier is the one in charge. This setup can cause low reliability, frustration, and high costs. Nevertheless, if the business or customer is able to control the source codes, they will be able to take their business to whatever service provider they want.

Is it necessary to use Open Source solutions?

Not really. Currently, the United Kingdom does not mandate the usage of Open Source solutions. They merely require it to be given equal and fair consideration as part of their procurement exercise. Nevertheless, you still have to consider using these solutions if you have them. Evaluate them accordingly and fairly. You should base your decisions on VfM. You should also implement solutions that provide the best VfM. In the event that the two solutions seem to be equal, then the government suggests that you choose the Open Source solution.

Does Open Source have a license?

Yes, it does. The copyright law protects software. The Open Source software is not exempted from this. Take note that using OSS comes with certain obligations. Not every license is the same and you have to carefully check it in order to know how you and your organization are allowed to use the software, such as publishing changes.

What are the security implications you have to consider when it comes to using Open Source solutions?

Open Source solution security implications are actually the same as those of proprietary software. Keep in mind that there is no specific type of software that is more or less secure than another. Likewise, there is no specific type of software that is more favorable than another. You have to consider each and every one of them on a case by case basis.

How can you obtain Open Source software?

The government requires a level playing field for all Open Source solutions. Hence, you have to read the documents that come with your toolkit.

Is it true that proprietary software is better supported as compared to Open Source software?

Not really. Some proprietary software versions are already outdated. They are not supported anymore.

Are Open Source software solutions really worthy to be considered?

Yes. In fact, you can find Open Source solutions that can be excellent alternatives to Open Office and other major proprietary software products.

So, Open Source software is not merely a fad?

It definitely is not a fad. Open Source software solutions have been available since the 1990s and they are here to stay.

If a certain department makes use of Open Source solutions, can everyone else access and modify the source code?

It actually depends on the license of the Open Source software. Theoretically, however, anyone can access and modify the source code since it is available for public use. Then again, it is still expected for departments to have a capable team designated to do this. So if you do not possess the necessary clearance or rights to access and modify the source code, then you will not be able to access and modify the source code. This does not necessarily violate or contradict the license concept of the Open Source solutions.

What does copyleft mean?

As you have learned from the previous chapter, copyleft is a concept created by Richard Stallman to serve as an alternative to copyright. It guarantees that materials are allowed to be used, examined, copied, built upon, and adapted freely. It is basically a form of licensing that can be used for maintaining copyright conditions for certain works, including art, software, and documents. Generally, the law of copyrights is used by authors to prevent other people from adapting, distributing, or reproducing copies of their work. So in contrast, copyleft allows authors to allow other people to adopt, distribute, or reproduce their work.

Let us say you developed a software program and released it under a GNU General Public License. Then, another person has modified that software program and decides to distribute the modified version. This modified version has to have a license under the GNU General Public License. Any other code specifically created to go with the modified version has to be licensed as well. With this being said, both the modified and the original versions are Open Source and the copyleft merely guarantees that the property is disseminated to every downstream derivative.

Take note that majority of the copyleft licenses you will find are Open Source. Then again, not every Open Source license is copyleft. This means that once a software program is released under this license, it gives other people permission to use it as a part of a program that is distributed under another license, such as a non-open source or proprietary license. Furthermore, the provisions on copyleft only apply to derivatives or cases in which there has been a modified copyleft work. Simply distributing copyleft works along with non-copyleft works does not really cause the non-copyleft works to be classified under the terms of copyleft.

How are businesses able to earn money from using Open Source?

A business can sell a service based on its code, warranty, or any other assurance. It can also offer maintenance and customization, as well as trademark license among others. Royalties or sales based on monopoly are actually the only type of profit strategy that does not go well with Open Source.

Does an Open Source software framework exists?

No. The government does not produce a framework or an approved list that allows purchases to be made for suppliers of Open Source. In order to abide by their policy, all new frameworks intended for the procurement of software is open to the suppliers of closed and open products. At present, you will not find any pre-selected or approved list of Open Source software, even though it is expected for certain OS products to be included in the Cloud Store.

Which Open Source solutions can be used?

Theoretically, all software solutions available can be used, provided that you have undertaken an options analysis as well as verified that the Open Source solution indeed meets the requirements of your department.

Can you download and source Open Source solutions on your computer?

It is not really expected for individuals to be able to download and source software or solutions, including Open Source, that do not match the standards given by the government. So if you wish to download and source any Open Source software solution on your home computer, you may do so. However, when you are at the office, you may not be able to do it unless you are an authorized developer.

Where can you find Open Source?

You have to read the document included in your toolkit to see examples of software or solutions. Take note that these solutions are neither endorsed nor approved by Home Office.

If Open Source is so good, then why it is given away for free?

Well, it is believed that the more people work on it, the better outcome will result. There would be better software since there would be people to fix and modify it. Users will be able to benefit from the past works of other people.

Are there any Open Source projects available?

Yes, there are. Some of these projects include the Linux Terminal Server Project, which aims to recycle or continue using obsolete hardware; OpenGroupware, which may eventually replace MS Exchange; and Jhai Foundation, which aims to use wireless footcrank-powered solid state Linux computers as well as bring Internet and telephony to Laos.

Chapter 9: Copyright versus Copyleft

Microsoft Windows XP EULA

According to Microsoft, you have the rights to comply with the conditions and terms of the Microsoft Windows XP EULA with regard to the following:

- *Use and installation.* You are allowed to use, install, display, run, and access a copy of this product on your computer, whether it is a workstation, a terminal, or any other device. However, this product is not allowed to be used by more than a couple of processors at any given time on your computer or Workstation Computer. Nonetheless, you are allowed to use ten computers or any other electronic devices to connect to your Workstation Computer. Indirect connections are included in this maximum number via multiplexing, hardware, or software that aggregates or pools connections. Unless permitted otherwise, you are not allowed to use this product on any device with the intention to display, run, or access executable software that is found on your Workstation Computer. You are also not allowed to use any device for the purpose of accessing, using, displaying, or running this product and its user interface, unless you have a separate license for your device.
- *Rights reservation.* Microsoft has every right not granted to you expressly in the EULA.
- *Transfer-Internal.* This product may be moved to another Workstation Computer. Once the transfer is done, you have to remove the product completely from your previous Workstation Computer. This is known as Transfer to Third Party. As the first user, you can make a one-time transfer to another user. Such transfer, however, must include every component part, printed material, media, the EULA, and a Certificate of Authenticity. Take note that this transfer is not permitted to be an indirect transfer like a consignment. Before this transfer, the person who acts as the end user should also agree to the terms of the EULA. Keep in mind that renting is strictly not allowed. You cannot rent, lend, lease, or offer commercial hosting services to any third party.
- *Limitations on disassembly, reverse engineering, and decompilation.* You are not allowed to disassemble, reverse engineer, or decompile this product, unless you are permitted by law.
- *Termination.* Microsoft has the right to cancel the EULA, without any prejudice to rights, if you do not follow the conditions and terms stated in

the EULA. In case the EULA is cancelled, you have to get rid of all your copies of this product along with its components.

Preamble to GNU Public License, 1991 Version 2

The licenses of majority of the software programs available are specifically designed to prevent you from sharing and changing it. In contrast to this, the GNU General Public License is meant to make sure that you are free to change and share software programs that are available for free. This is to ensure that such software remains free of charge for everyone.

When it comes to free software, take note that it refers to the freedom and not the price. General Public Licenses are actually designed to ensure that you are free to give away copies of the free software as well as charge a price for your service in case you decide to modify it. In order to keep your rights protected, restrictions should be made with regard to forbidding other people from denying you your rights as well as asking you to give them up. These restrictions apply when you decide to distribute copies of modify the software.

For instance, if you give away copies of the program, you have to provide your end users the same rights that you own. You have to guarantee that they can also acquire the source code for the program. In addition, you have to tell them about the terms and conditions, so they will be aware of their rights.

As a user, your rights are protected via software copyright and a license that gives you permission to modify, copy, or distribute the software. Moreover, for every author protection, you have to make everybody understand that a warranty for such free software does not exist. In the event that somebody mentions the original version of the software, any problems that occur from such modification will not be attended to by the author.

Furthermore, a free program tends to be constantly threatened by software patents. This is why free program redistribution and obtaining patent license are aimed to be avoided by turning free programs into proprietary programs. Each patent has to either be licensed for the free use of everybody or does not have any license at all.

Chapter 10: Security

Open Source software security is basically the measure of guarantee or assurance in the freedom from risk and danger inherent to open source software solutions.

Open Algorithms and Open Source software

In general, software projects are an algorithm implementation. Even though implementations may only be tested and such testing only proves the existence of errors, algorithms may still be proven right.

If you think about it, a premise in its secret key cryptography is that an algorithm has to be known. Also, only a tiny piece of information should remain secret and that is the secret key. So in order for a cypher to be deemed secure, an algorithm has to be proven right and such proof has to be available to anyone who wishes to use this cypher.

Thus, when it comes to security of computers, algorithms have to be open. Nevertheless, there is still a continuing debate on whether or not implementations have to be proprietary or open source.

A Debate on Implementation

Trying to audit an implementation can be quite stressful and time-consuming. However, it can still be significantly reduced if you concentrate on proving that it indeed corresponds to a certain algorithm. This algorithm has to be proven right. Ideally, the auditor should be able to access the source code, whether it is proprietary or open source.

It is crucial to realize that software audit actually depends on source code access. With this being said, a new proprietary software audit basically depends on the readiness or willingness of the software owner. Open source software audit, on the other hand, may be done any time by anyone who is willing to do it.

Such concern has been more and more austere as backdoors in reputable software started to be disclosed. Because of this, the continuous debate with regard to the security of open source software has lost its meaning. It no longer matters if open source software improves or lessens its security.

Although certain arguments on both sides can be subjective and there isn't any relationship between application vulnerabilities and their proprietary or open source status that has been observed, they may still have backdoors. Then again, only the open source software may be audited freely. Thus, the proprietary software should be regarded as inherently not secure.

Advantages of Open Source Security

Open Source security has plenty of advantages. Here are some of them:

- A lot of people are allowed to check out the source code to look for a possible vulnerability and fix it. This may result in a quicker discovery of unintentional vulnerabilities in security as well as prevention of intentional backdoors or vulnerabilities in the source code. Take note that this may have been placed there by their developers.
- Users are forced by proprietary software to accept a security level that vendors are willing to offer as well as to accept the rates that updates and patches are released on the market.
- Open source code end users have the ability to modify and chance the source in order to implement extra security features that they may want to use for a specific purpose. They may even extend it to a kernel level that they want.
- It is always presumed that compilers are used to create codes that are trustworthy. However, as shown by Ken Thompson, compilers can be subverted with a Thompson hack to produce faulty executables, which are produced unwittingly by good developers. When a developer gains access to the compiler's source code, he also gains the ability to find out whether or not there is any mal-intention.
- Another demonstration by David Wheeler also proves that there are two different self-compiling compilers that are open source. These compilers must have the capability to compile each other as well as be used for establishing binaries for one of them.
- The Kerckhoff's principle is based upon the principle that enemies can steal secure military systems and not compromise their acquired information. This idea has become a basis for a lot of contemporary security practices, most of which are practiced today. In addition, it is said that security through obscurity is actually a bad practice.

Disadvantages of Open Source Security

As you have read from previous chapters, there are many advantages to using Open Source software solutions. At the same time, however, there are many disadvantages to using it as well. Here are some of them:

- Attackers would find it easier to spot vulnerabilities in the source code.
- When you make the source code available, it does not immediately guarantee review. For instance, when security system design and implementation expert Marcus Ranum released a public firewall toolkit, only ten individuals provided him with patches or feedback. There were more than two thousand sites that used his toolkit, but only a handful gave a response.
- Many eyes that review a code can trick users into having a false sense of security. Keep in mind that having a lot of users view source codes does not exactly ensure that the security flaws are going to be spotted and fixed.

Models and Metrics

There are various models and metrics that measure a system's security. Some of the methods used in measuring software system security include the following:

The number of days in between the vulnerabilities

Many people argue that systems are at their most vulnerable state when there is a potential vulnerability spotted prior to a path being created. So when you measure the number of days in between such vulnerability and then fixed it, you will be able to determine a basis on the system's security. Also, take note that there are certain caveats to this approach. You have to realize that not all vulnerabilities are equally negative. Fixing many bugs in a short period of time may also not be better than merely finding a handful and taking a while longer to fix. You may want to put more importance to the effectiveness of the fix as well as your operating system.

The Poisson process

You can use it to measure different rates that pertain to how individuals find flaws in security when it comes to using closed source and open source software solutions. This process can be further broken down into the number of paid viewers and volunteers.

The Morningstar model

When you compare a huge variety of closed source and open source solutions, you can also use a star system to analyze the security of projects just like the way

Morningstar rates mutual funds. Once you have set a huge enough data, you can use statistics to measure the total effectiveness of a particular group over another.

The coverity scan

Stanford University has collaborated with Coverity to establish a baseline for open source security and quality. This recent development is done with the help of the Department of Homeland Security. Innovations with regard to automated defect detection are used to identify bugs in software programs. The level of security and quality is typically measured using rungs, which do not really have an exact definition. It can also change when Coverity produces new tools.

Conclusion

Thank you again for downloading this book!

I hope this book was able to help you to understand better the concept of open source and its benefits to the public.

Finally, if you enjoyed this book, please take the time to share your thoughts and post a review on Amazon. It'd be greatly appreciated!

Thank you and good luck!